BRITAIN

According to

VERY
BRITISH
PROBLEMS

BRITAIN

According to

VERY
BRITISH
PROBLEMS

ROB TEMPLE

SPHERE

SPHERE

First published in Great Britain in 2024 by Sphere

5 7 9 10 8 6 4

Copyright © Rob Temple 2024
Illustrations © Shutterstock

A CIP catalogue record for this book
is available from the British Library.

ISBN 978-1-4087-3399-8

Typeset in Caslon by M Rules
Printed and bound in Great Britain by
Clays Ltd, Elcograf S.p.A.

Papers used by Sphere are from well-managed forests
and other responsible sources.

MIX
Paper | Supporting
responsible forestry
FSC® C104740

Sphere
An imprint of
Little, Brown Book Group
Carmelite House
50 Victoria Embankment
London EC4Y 0DZ

The authorised representative
in the EEA is
Hachette Ireland
8 Castlecourt Centre
Dublin 15, D15 XTP3, Ireland
(email: info@hbgi.ie)

An Hachette UK Company
www.hachette.co.uk

www.littlebrown.co.uk

To Sumin

INTRODUCTION

Welcome, dear reader, to a whimsical expedition across Britain, taking in all that's quirky, quaint and curious along the way. In this uproarious tome, we embark on a rollicking journey from A to Z, with a pit stop at your preferred motorway service station when we're all feeling in dire need of a restorative cuppa.

We'll explore the idiosyncrasies, eccentricities and downright absurdities that make Britain the charmingly peculiar place it is. From Abbey Road to zebra crossings (see what I did there?), we'll traverse the length and breadth of these splendid isles, pausing along the way to uncover delightful facts and curious tales, all served, naturally, with jam, cream and a healthy dollop of irreverent British humour.

I will be your guide. I feel somewhat qualified (not to boast, heaven forbid) as for over a decade I've been obsessed with Britain, this little patch of land I call home. With Very British Problems on social media, over the past twelve years – gosh, time flies – I've amassed over five million awkward followers, who I'm very fond of by the way, and together we diligently explore what truly makes the British tick. We British have so many curious customs, cherished traditions and unique turns of phrase, and more baffling etiquette than you can shake a stick at – not to mention delicious food and drink – so I felt it was high time I picked my favourites to put together in one glorious place.

You can use this book for many things: 1. It's perfect for swotting up/pillaging for your next pub quiz (see the Q section for quizzes, or indeed the P section for pubs). 2. Take it away with you on holiday to read on the beach and remind you of home (or use it on one of Britain's own beautiful wind-swept beaches, some of which are mentioned in this book). 3. If you're a visitor to Britain, use it as a study guide so you know how to blend in (see how to eat biscuits in the B section, or how to queue properly in the Q section). 4. Put it on your bedside table to gently chuckle yourself to sleep. 5. Read it on the underground (U section) to help you to avoid eye contact with fellow passengers. 6. Put it over your head when you forget your umbrella (also the U section, and see the W section too for weather).

So, mind the gap, don your light jacket, fasten your seatbelt, fetch your flask of tea, and prepare to smile politely as we embark (chocks away!) on a delightful ramble through the charming oddities of British life. For this is Britain! According to Very British Problems.

Let the adventure commence.

Rob Temple, Cambridge

A

Afternoon Tea

Tea is cheap. Sandwiches are cheap (especially when the main ingredient is cucumber). Now, Afternoon Tea is a clever way that posh hotels have found to combine the two to make them very expensive. Still, as indulgent treats go, there's possibly no better way to pass a large chunk of the day.

Angel of the North

Contemporary sculpture by Antony Gormley, located in Gateshead, completed in 1998. It's believed to be the largest sculpture of an angel in the world and is viewed by an estimated 33 million people a year, a lot of them while driving on the A1. If you pass it heading north, you know you're about to start seeing people wearing short sleeves in minus temperatures.

Apples

Keeping the doctor away from Brits for centuries. Around 7,000 varieties of apple exist in the world, and over 2,500 of those varieties have been developed in the UK. Britain's bestselling apple: Gala.

Aggression (passive)

Brits are the world leaders in passive aggression. If you encounter any of the following statements from a Brit, either in person or via email, you're being assaulted:

- With all due respect ...
- As per my last email ...

- Polite notice . . .
- Thanks in advance . . .
- As previously mentioned . . .
- Not sure if you received my message . . .
- When you're ready . . .
- In your own time . . .
- Maybe I'm not being clear . . .
- Happy to discuss . . .
- Thanks anyway . . .
- An email ending in 'Regards' when 'Kind regards' has been used in a preceding email.

Abbey Road

Street in north-west London that's home to Abbey Road Studios and the famous zebra crossing (see the Z section for more on zebra crossings) immortalised by the Beatles (see the B section for more on the Beatles) on the cover of their 1969 album, *Abbey Road*. When you've reached a point in life when you can make road markings popular tourist destinations simply by walking on them – the crossing has Grade II listed building status – then, well, you've done all right for yourself.

Angel Delight

Powdered dessert mix introduced by Bird's (see Victoria Sponge in the V section for more on Alfred Bird) in 1967, sold in strawberry, butterscotch, chocolate and banana flavours. Named Britain's favourite childhood dish in 2015 by Food Network. Tastes like fluffy clouds that have had sugar thrown on them by fairies. Well, from what I remember, anyway.

Aberdeen

There are over thirty 'Aberdeens' in the world, but we're here for the distinguished spot in Scotland. It's home to the royal estate of Balmoral, Scotland's oldest bridge – the 700-year-old Brig O'Balgownie – and is said to be the UK's luckiest place, with over forty-seven lottery millionaires made in Aberdeenshire. Pardon me while I embark on an eight-hour drive northward just to try my luck with a scratchcard.

Abergavenny

Market town in Monmouthshire, Wales. Promoted as a Gateway to Wales, as it's six miles from the English border. A perfect place from which to explore the Brecon Beacons.

Alan Turing

Father of modern computer science and decoder of German Enigma machines during World War II. Features on the £50 note.

Albert Hall (Royal)

Concert hall in South Kensington, London, opened by Queen Victoria in 1871. Hosts more than 390 shows in the main auditorium every year, including the iconic BBC Proms. In some variants of the 1939 novelty song, 'Hitler Has Only Got One Ball', the dictator's missing testicle is said to reside here, although I've visited numerous times and am yet to see it.

'Ah well, never mind'

What a Brit says when all of their dreams are crushed.

Argos

Established in 1972, this iconic British retailer gained renown for its innovative catalogue ordering system, which captivated customers with the ritual of using little red pencils to fill in order forms in an otherwise empty room. However, in 2020, Argos ceased printing paper catalogues. I found this a shame as I'm British and therefore don't like change.

Alton Towers

The premier theme park in Britain, with 1.8 million visitors to its Staffordshire location each year. Home to rides such as Oblivion, Runaway Mine Train, The Smiler and Nemesis. The grounds, which were once used as an officer training unit during World War II, were opened to the public in the 1950s and featured a mini railway which visitors could pay to view. In the 1960s and 1970s, a boating lake and a chairlift were introduced, and in 1980, the installation of The Corkscrew rollercoaster, the Pirate Ship, and the Alpine Bobsled ride began the estate's evolution into a modern theme park. My ambition in life is to one day manage to visit when it's not raining.

Asparagus

From 23 April (St George's Day) to 21 June (summer solstice) it's asparagus season in Britain, making the nation's wee smell funny for eight and a half weeks. Fun fact: Asparagus can grow up to 25cm within a twenty-four-hour period.

B

Biscuits

I could fill a whole book with biscuit talk, but I have to be brief, so I'll simply list the ten British rules of biscuits:

1. When opening a packet, any broken biscuits must be consumed immediately.
2. Never dunk a biscuit for too long; you will ruin both your biscuit and your tea. Double sadness.

3. Always offer biscuits to guests, even if they claim they're not interested (they're probably fibbing).
4. Don't be the person who snatches the last biscuit of a kind unless you're prepared to face the consequences – i.e., a new enemy.
5. Always offer a hot drink with biscuits, obviously.
6. Bring out a posh selection of biscuits (metal tin, two layers separated by a sheet of springy purple cardboard, usually called a 'collection') for special occasions.
7. Always pretend you haven't seen a plate of biscuits being passed around until they're offered to you, then act pleasantly surprised.
8. Utilise the phrases 'I really mustn't', 'Ooh, go on then' and 'If you're having one'.
9. Wrap biscuits up when not in use, either by pushing the open packet up against a wall, or by using a jar, tin or box.
10. Always have more biscuits in stock than you think you need. Never run out. Running out of biscuits is like running out of air: not ideal.

Blackpool Tower

Visit on a sunny day, if you can. I went up on a foggy day. Like looking into a steam room. Asked for my money back – no joy.

Bread Rolls

Is a bread roll even called a bread roll, though? Or is it a cob? Or a barm? Or a bun? Or a bap? Or a batch, stotty, teacake or muffin? Or a bara or a scuffler? (For any southerners reading, I didn't just make those last two up, I swear.) Answer: It's all of them, it just depends on where you're from. Britain: such a small place, such a ridiculously large selection of names for bread products.

The Beatles

John, Paul, George and Ringo, four Liverpudlians who created the best band of all time. Had their first

Number 1 hit in 1963 and their last one (at time of writing) in 2023. Some people will tell you they don't 'get' the Beatles – these people are not to be trusted.

Baked Beans

British people will look at a food – any food (even baked beans) – and the first thought that'll pop into their minds will be: 'I wonder if I could put baked beans on that.' Quite often the answer is yes, if the Heinz Beanz Pizza (yes, it's a real product you can get in shops) is anything to go by.

Bean (Mr)

There's often an argument on social media as to whether Mr Bean, played by Rowan Atkinson, is an angel or an alien. In my opinion, he's just a very funny, odd man. And one with worldwide appeal due to his mostly non-verbal exploits. Unbelievably, there were only fifteen episodes, from 1990–5, despite it feeling like there were about 200.

Big Ben

'It's the name of the bell, the tower is called The Elizabeth Tower!' I already hear some Brits screaming before I've even said anything. Completed in 1859, it's the third tallest clock tower in the UK, after the Joseph Chamberlain Memorial Clock Tower (Birmingham) and the Royal Liver Building (Liverpool). The bell (called Big Ben) arrived in London by barge on the Thames and was taken across Westminster Bridge by a carriage drawn by sixteen white horses. And the musical note it plays when struck? E.

Brown Sauce

The only sauce of choice for a sausage sandwich.

Birmingham

The UK's 'second city'. Birthplace of many other Bs that could be in this section: the balti, Black Sabbath,

Blinders (Peaky) – see below, the Baskerville font, the bicycle bell. And also many things that don't begin with B, such as the postage stamp, the electric kettle, X-rays, the weather map and the vacuum cleaner. What's more, Brummie Conway Berners-Lee was part of the team which produced the Ferranti Mark 1 in 1951, the first commercially available electronic computer. His son, Tim (who you'll find in the T section), invented a little thing called the World Wide Web.

Blinders (Peaky)

Six-season drama set in Birmingham, created by Steven Knight, following the exploits of a crime gang in the aftermath of World War I. Inspired many, many British men to get a rather severe haircut, wear a flat cap, and then feel sad when they realised they weren't as good-looking as Cillian Murphy.

Barbecues

Has the temperature crept above 14 degrees Celsius? If so, Brits will rush to the nearest supermarket, purchase all the sausages and rush home again to burn them over some charcoal on the Weber BBQ that's usually covered in last year's grime ('It just burns itself off, don't worry'). My favourite task during a barbecue: standing next to the person actually doing the barbecuing and occasionally saying, 'That one needs turning, I think.'

Boxing Day

Best day of the year. Involves eating leftover sandwiches, munching chocolate and reading that funny book you got for Christmas (I see you).

Ben Nevis

Highest mountain in Scotland. In fact, one viral Tripadvisor review called it out for being 'Very Steep and Too High' and for not having a restaurant at the summit, so be warned.

Borough Market

Innocently wander into this market in Southwark, London, and wander out again in twenty minutes now

£35 lighter because you somehow bought three blocks of fancy cheese without even realising.

Brexit

Actually, let's just leave it ...

C

Custard Cream

Yes, we've already mentioned biscuits in the B section, but this, my personal favourite biscuit, must get a standalone entry. Originating in Britain in 1908, I'd argue the custard cream is far superior to its chocolatey cousin, the bourbon, and in a Very British Problems poll of 27,596 people, 54 per cent of you agreed – hurrah!

Cornwall

Picturesque beaches, coastlines, pasties and the 'jam first' method of scone layering. Any Cornish folks reading this will wonder why it's featuring in a book about Britain when, they'll argue, Cornwall is a separate country of its own.

'Could do'

A British person absolutely adores saying 'Could do,' which roughly translates as: 'No.' Other phrases Brits use that mean 'No':

- 'We'll see.'
- 'Well, yes and no.'
- 'I'm easy really.'
- 'I'll see how I feel.'
- 'I might do.'
- 'I'll think about it.'
- 'Let's talk about it later.'

Celebrities

Thanks to social media and reality TV (see the L section for *Love Island*), around 98 per cent of British people now count as celebrities. In fact, if you're one of the 2 per cent of normal bog-standard folks, you're an exceedingly rare breed, which kind of makes you ... a bit of a celebrity.

Cozzie Livs

Hopefully the Cozzie Livs (cost of living crisis)
will have gone away a bit by the time you're reading
this, but let's not get into that – this entry is purely
to demonstrate how much Britain loves silly
abbreviations. The Queen's Platinum Jubilee became
Platty Joobs, holidays have long been known as
holibobs, a bottomless brunch became a Botty B and,
I'm told (I need to be told youth slang because I'm
old now), a nervous breakdown became a Nervy B –
how fun!

Clocks

British people can never believe how light it is in the
evenings when the clocks go forward, and they can
never believe how dark it is when the clocks go back.
Despite it happening every year without fail, the
strength of these disbeliefs will never dissipate.

Christmas

Brits can also never believe it's nearly Christmas,
which, in Britain, now starts in mid-July. It's the time

of year when Brits live on mince pies and Quality Street (see the Q section), have our annual portion of turkey, pretend to like mulled drinks, gather all the family to viciously fall out over a game of Monopoly and give each other stocking fillers such as this book you're reading right now.

The Cotswolds

Nestled in the heart of England like a cosy cashmere blanket, this picturesque region is a postcard come to life. Here, villages with names straight out of a fairy tale – think Bourton-on-the-Water and Lower Slaughter – charm visitors with their honey-coloured stone cottages and friendly locals, who welcome you into their cafés and then charge you £8.50 for an organic rhubarb lemonade (200ml).

Cricket

The best game to watch while eating sandwiches. If you know the rules from childhood, they're simple and make perfect sense, but if you come to them new as an adult, they're the most baffling set of nonsense (silly mid-on? googly?) ever invented. The game is believed to have originated in south-east England in medieval times, but underwent major development in the eighteenth century to become England's national sport. Is it an interesting sport to watch? Well, I think so. But then again, I like going to the garden centre to look at sheds.

Cheese

According to The British Cheese Board (absolutely genius name) there are over 700 named British cheeses produced in the UK. And the UK's favourite cheese is another for this C category: the mighty Cheddar.

Crisps

Britain is a land of crisps. In fact, according to data from Leicestershire-based crisp giant Walkers, 98 per cent of UK adults – that's 52.9 million people – identify themselves as 'crisp eaters'. You wonder what that other 2 per cent are playing at. But do we prefer Cheese & Onion or Salt & Vinegar? According to a Very British Problems poll of 23,166 people, Salt & Vinegar takes the crown with 54 per cent of the vote.

Cashpoints

The world's first cashpoint was put into use by Barclays Bank in Enfield on 27 June 1967. Since then Brits have been furtively looking around while entering their PIN, causing everyone queueing behind them to politely look in every direction but that of the machine. Them's the rules.

Cardiff

The capital and largest city of Wales. Fun fact: The city is home to Spillers, the oldest record store in the world, dating back to 1894. It used to sell wax records for the newly invented phonograph.

Cows

Brits can't drive past a cow without saying 'cow'. I've no idea why.

Conkers

In the days before smartphones, British children used to gather conkers in autumn, attach them to shoelaces and smack them against each other. To toughen up their conkers, some would put them in the freezer, some would soak them in vinegar, some would put them in the airing cupboard, and some would even varnish them. I recently told this to a teenager, who looked up from TikTok just long enough to reply, 'What are you going on about, bro?'

Crumpets

Why are crumpets so good? Let me put a question to you: Is there another food that so perfectly traps melted butter? Case closed.

D

Dinner

Or perhaps tea? The eternal debate among Brits, each
with a different answer influenced by their upbringing
and regional roots. Much like the age-old preferences
of which side of the bed to sleep on or where to
sit around the dinner (or tea) table, once you've
determined whether you're a dinner person or a tea
person, there's simply no turning back.

Dancing on Ice

A show in which celebrities learn to dance on an ice
rink. Many go bum over tit and hurt themselves,
while some eventually get the hang of it. Watched by
millions.

Downing Street (10)

Official residence of the prime minister of the United Kingdom. Situated in Whitehall in the City of Westminster, the Grade I listed building is over 300 years old and contains approximately 100 rooms. While some leaders have made Number 10 their home for extended periods – such as William Pitt the Younger, who resided there for an impressive twenty years, more than any other PM – others, like Liz Truss, barely had time to unpack a saucepan.

Doctor Who

No list of iconic British treasures is complete without the time-and-space-travelling Doctor. Since 1963, fifteen actors have embodied the enigmatic Time Lord, enchanting audiences with tales of adventure, heroism and a uniquely British style of surreal daftness.

Daffodils

Daffodils, the harbinger of spring, are a cheerful sight adorning British homes once sunnier weather is in sight. Often purchased by the £1 bunch at supermarket checkouts. Additionally, they hold special significance as the national flower of Wales, proudly worn on St David's Day (1 March) to celebrate Welsh heritage and culture.

David Attenborough (Sir)

Esteemed British broadcaster and naturalist, whose distinctive voice and unparalleled storytelling has inspired millions to cherish our planet's biodiversity and ecosystems. YouGov even officially crowned him the nation's favourite personality. If scientists unlock the secret to eternal life, we'd humbly request they administer the magic pill to Sir David first.

Duxford Imperial War Museum

Airfield in Cambridgeshire boasting Britain's largest aviation collection, which spans over 200 aircraft and military vehicles housed within seven expansive exhibition buildings. I'd go there every weekend if I could, it's only down the road from me, but if I did I expect my wife would leave me.

Del Boy

Derek Trotter, beloved fictional character from the BBC sitcom *Only Fools and Horses*, is renowned for delivering some of the most iconic comedy lines in television history, such as 'It's a well-known fact that 90 per cent of all foreign tourists come from abroad' and 'He was about as useful as a pair of sunglasses on a bloke with one ear.'

DFS

Has it got a sale on at the minute? Let me just check ... OF COURSE IT HAS!

Double-decker Buses

To Brits, snagging the front seats on the top deck feels akin to piloting a spaceship – utterly exhilarating. You can achieve a similar high by sitting at the front of London's first driverless trains on the DLR (Docklands Light Railway) which opened in 1987. However, the allure diminishes considerably for the rest of the seats. To tourists, double-deckers are symbolic of Britain itself. Single-level coaches just don't cut it in comparison. I mean, I've seen plenty of visitors to Britain taking pictures of double-decker buses, but I've never seen anyone rushing to take a snap of a coach trip to Scunthorpe.

Derbyshire

County in the East Midlands of England, home to Derby (obviously), Bakewell (lovely tarts) and Buxton (lovely water), as well as most of the Peak District.

If someone from Derbyshire calls you 'duck' don't worry, you've not turned into a mallard, it's a term of endearment.

Devon

I just remembered I'd put Cornwall in this book and suddenly imagined the uproar if I left out cream-first Devon, so here's an entry for Devon.

E

Eccentricity

Britain is a tad barmy, and all the better for it.
Where else can you chase a big cheese down a hill or
partake in a pancake race (see the P section for more
details)? Where else can you witness the World Bog
Snorkelling Championships or spot Morris dancers
jigging around on a village green? This is the country
that boasts a political party called The Official Monster
Raving Loony Party. Eccentricity isn't just tolerated;
it's celebrated, whether it's Monty Python's Flying
Circus, Willy Wonka, Mr Bean, or Mr Blobby. From
Doctor Who to The Mad Hatter, Britain embraces
the whimsical and unconventional with open arms.
The country is a tapestry of oddities and quirks, and,
personally, I wouldn't have it any other way.

Ely

The name of the Cambridgeshire city is derived from the Northumbrian word 'elge', meaning 'district of eels'. Couldn't leave a fact like that out of this book. And talking of eels ...

Eels (jellied)

East End of London culinary delicacy. If you like fish but wish it was slimier and wobblier, this is the snack for you.

EastEnders

Soap opera that's been chronicling the lives of the residents of fictional borough Walford in London's East End since dinosaurs roamed the earth (actually since 1985 but feels longer). The reason you can tell it's fiction is because humble market traders reside in palatial London townhouses (yet can't afford a washing machine, instead using a laundrette), when, in reality, finding a room under £2,000 a month in zone 2 in London is like discovering a unicorn in your garage.

Eton College

Public boarding school for boys in Berkshire, known for its wealth and notable alumni. With a staggering twenty British prime ministers among its graduates, one might say this institution, for better or worse, holds a significant share of responsibility for shaping the course of British history.

Eton Mess

No, not Boris Johnson, but a delicious dessert consisting of strawberries, meringue and cream. First mentioned in 1893, it originated at Eton College and is served at the annual cricket match against the pupils of Harrow School.

Egg and Cress Sandwiches

There's always someone eating one on the train. Always. I even saw someone open one in a busy lift once. Ridiculous behaviour.

Edinburgh

Capital city of Scotland and the seventh-most-populous city in the UK. Fun facts: 1. A lot of *Harry Potter* was filmed in Edinburgh. 2. Over 75 per cent of the city's buildings are listed. 3. It's home to the Edinburgh Festival Fringe, the world's largest performance arts festival, surpassed by only the Olympics and the FIFA World Cup in terms of global ticketed events.

EasyJet

Budget-friendly British airline offering remarkably low fares. And once you've bought a ticket to Barcelona for £17, all you then have to do is pay a little extra for things like luggage, meals, priority boarding, seat selection . . . Oh, suddenly your ticket costs £350. Bargain.

Eccles Cakes

Sweet pastries filled with currants, sugar and spices, originating in the town of Eccles in Greater Manchester. Enjoyed as a popular snack in Britain since the eighteenth century. Are they nicer than Bakewell tarts, though?

Elgar

Celebrated composer who left an indelible mark on British history through his stirring compositions. His iconic works, including 'Pomp and Circumstance Marches' and 'Nimrod' from the 'Enigma Variations', evoke a sense of national pride and identity and remain an enduring symbol of British cultural heritage. He was also the bloke with the huge moustache on the £20 note from 2007–2010.

Easter Egg Mugs

In the old days, an Easter egg wasn't just chocolate; it came with a mug that became a lifelong treasure. Nearly every Brit over thirty-five has a cupboard boasting a mug adorned with a British confectionery logo. I'm currently sipping tea from my beloved Smarties mug – if it ever broke, I'd need counselling.

F

Fish and Chips

People flock to Britain's fish-filled shores from all over the world to sample this crispy beige delight. British chip shops boast some brilliantly imaginative names, such as Codrophenia, A Fish Called Rhonda, Frying Nemo, and The Cod Almighty. An unspoken rule dictates that upon entering a chippie, one must gaze up at the menu, squinting, as if debating what to have, before inevitably choosing the same thing every single time. To be a proper Brit, one must also, at a young age, decide what type of chip-topping person one is:

- Gravy: You're no-nonsense, you go out in a short-sleeve shirt in winter – probably a northerner.

- Curry sauce: Ooh, look at you, a bit flamboyant, you like a bit of excitement in life.
- Just salt and vinegar: You're a traditionalist, you're over fifty, you sensibly bring a heat-saving 'bag for life' to carry your food home in.
- Cheese: You're twenty-two and drunk.
- Mayonnaise: You're actually from Belgium.

(Deep)-Fried Mars Bar

Since it originated in Aberdeen in the 1990s, the deep-fried Mars Bar has been a popular novelty item in Scottish chip shops. I had one for the first time in 2012 and I'm still enjoying digesting it to this day.

Football

A Brit must choose a team to support as soon as they're old enough to speak, for one (or more) of three reasons:

1. You're born near the team.
2. Your family tells you to.
3. You like the colour of the team's kit.

And then that's it, you're stuck with that team for the rest of your life. Not too bad if you're lucky enough to be born in, say, Manchester, or London, but spare a thought for poor sods like me: I was born in Peterborough.

Frome

This town in Somerset was named as the 'sixth coolest town' in Britain by *The Times* in 2014 and the best place to live in the south-west by the *Sunday Times* in 2018 and 2021, suggesting there's an editor at *The Times* who happens to be from Frome. Former F1 driving ace Jenson Button was born in Frome and has a street – Jenson Avenue – named after him, as well as a bridge – the Jenson Button Bridge. He was also awarded the freedom of the town in 2010. Where does he live now? That's right . . . California.

Funny Place Names

How about I just list a small selection of funny British place names (real ones!) and you can giggle for a bit in a puerile way? Okay, here you go: Wetwang. Blubberhouses. Curry Mallet. Mudford Sock. Queen Camel. Barton in the Beans. Sandy Balls. Prickwillow. Shitterton. Fanny Hands Lane. Giggleswick. Crapstone. Droop. Brokenwind. Twatt.

'Funny, that!'

If something happens and it was fully expected and predicted by a Brit, they will always celebrate by saying 'Funny, that!' in a sarcastic way. We can't resist. Example: You warned it would rain and the person didn't listen. They come inside holding their chair cushions and say, 'Oh no, they're all wet.' You now smile and say: 'Funny, that!'

Fry-ups

Brits will fight over what does and does not go on a fry-up, with perhaps the most contentious area of debate: do the beans go straight on the plate, or in a little ceramic pot?

Furniture Village

If you want to observe British couples who have firmly passed the honeymoon stage, come to Furniture Village in a British retail park on a grey Saturday afternoon. Perhaps you'll then stroll into Home Bargains, and on to Currys to browse the mouse mats, and finally to Costa Coffee for a warm latte and a serviceable tuna melt. A classic British way to spend a precious day off in this one short life we're given.

The Fens

The Fens are 1,500 square miles of very flat marshy area spanning Lincolnshire, Cambridgeshire, Norfolk and Suffolk. One of the richest arable areas in the UK. Life is pretty quiet in the Fens (I should know, I've lived in them most of my life). This lack of excitement leads to events such as the World Peashooting Championship, held in the village of Witcham, springing into existence. Or the Whittlesey Straw Bear Festival, where each year on Plough Tuesday, a man or a boy is covered head to toe in straw and led from house to house. Then that boy is never seen again (just kidding).

Ferries

Surrounded by water, Brits are no strangers to a ferry. If you've never been on one, imagine a motorway service station, but it's on the sea so it's wobbly and you're stuck in it for ages.

G

Greggs

Purveyor of affordable baked goods on every high street. The sausage rolls (both regular and vegan) for which the chain is most famous (though sometimes I have a chicken bake when I feel my life needs excitement) are, in my experience, either straight from the oven and therefore hotter than magma, one bite causing one to lose a whole layer of mouth, or they're stone cold. I'm yet to experience a temperature between these two extremes, though I will keep trying. Yes, I will try multiple times a day.

Guy Fawkes

We find it hard to let things go, we Brits. It's been over 400 years since the plot to blow up the Houses of Parliament on 5 November 1605, yet every year we put an effigy of conspirator Guy Fawkes on a bonfire and burn it to bits while setting off explosions in the sky. Imagine if Guy came back to life for just one day to witness a British fireworks display:

'See that, Guy?' <firework goes off, everyone goes 'Oooh'>

'Yeah?'

'That's about you, that is.'

'You're kidding?'

'Nope.'

'But it was over four hundred years ago!'

'I know.'

'Do you do a night like this for anyone else?'

'No, just you. Here, have a sparkler.'

Great British Bake Off

TV programme on which amateur bakers make cakes in a tent and then must go home if Paul Hollywood doesn't like the cakes. Watched by millions.

Glastonbury Festival

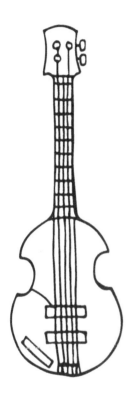

Around 200,000 people flock down to Pilton in Somerset each summer (apart from fallow years every half a decade or so for the land to recover) for the ultimate festival, combining music, comedy, dance, theatre, cabaret and stalls selling three falafels in a pita bread for £16.50. If you want to sing along to the best acts in the world, these are the fields to do it in. Personally, I prefer to watch it on the telly from the comfort of my own home due to festival toilets being about as messy and welcoming as the Battle of the Somme, but then I'm not very adventurous.

Grimsby

Port town in north-east Lincolnshire, once the home port for the world's largest fishing fleet around the mid-twentieth century. Its people are known as

Grimbarians. The top Google suggestion for questions about Grimsby is 'What does Grimsby smell like?'

Gogglebox

People watching people watching telly. Watched by millions.

Gordon Ramsay

Arguably the most famous chef in the world, known for catchphrases such as 'Damn', 'Wow' and 'F*** me, that's disgusting'. You can't really call yourself an amateur cook these days unless Chef Ramsay has personally taken you to one side of a busy kitchen and called you a donkey.

Gin

Causing laughter then tears up and down the country since the thirteenth century. Responsible for the 'Gin o'clock' (also 'Live Laugh Love') sign epidemic that started to spread across modern Britain around 2008 and which sees no sign of dissipating.

Great Fire of London

A fire (a great one), starting in Pudding Lane on Sunday 2 September, 1666, that swept through central London until the strong east wind dropped four days later. London was reconstructed on the same medieval street plan which still exists today, just with less wood this time.

George Orwell

English writer, 1903–50. Wrote *1984*, a much-lauded vision of the future, despite it failing to predict two of the key events in the actual 1984: 'Do They Know it's Christmas?' by Band Aid going to Number 1 and Everton winning the FA Cup. He also wrote his essay 'A Nice Cup of Tea' in the *Evening Standard*, listing eleven rules for the perfect cuppa. Bleak vision of dystopia . . . how to have a nice cup of tea . . . you can't accuse him of not being varied in his topics.

Getting There

Brits will say they're 'getting there', despite getting nowhere at all and even in some cases when they've noticeably regressed.

Garibaldi Biscuits

AKA squashed fly biscuits or dead fly biscuits, due to the layer of compressed fruit (usually currants or raisins) resembling squashed insects. Named after Giuseppe Garibaldi, an Italian general who made a popular visit to South Shields in 1854, the Garibaldi biscuit was first manufactured by Bermondsey biscuit company Peek Freans in 1861. But does Britain like them? Well, according to a 2024 Very British Problems poll of over 8,000 people, only 54 per cent said they'd eat one. Truly a divisive biscuit.

Greenwich Mean Time

Great time. Beautiful time. The best time. Lovely time. No other time like it. First class.

H

Happiness

Brits don't strictly 'do' happiness, instead we have these alternatives:

- Being not too bad.
- Being happy enough.
- Being not unhappy.
- Being fine, all things considered.
- Having no cause to complain.
- Muddling through.
- Trundling on.
- Living the dream.
- Being neither here nor there.
- Being all right, all things considered.
- Surviving.
- Being unhappy but used to it.

- Being still alive/not dead yet.
- Having ups and downs.
- Knowing that it could be worse.
- Being fair to middling.
- Saying 'Mustn't grumble.'
- Having your health.
- Admitting that 'It is what it is.'
- Being sure it'll be fine.

Heartbeat

Every British generation, especially those pre-Netflix, has a TV theme song that catapults them back to Sunday evenings in childhood (*Antiques Roadshow*, *Last of the Summer Wine*, *Songs of Praise*, *Ski Sunday*) inducing a sudden panic about unfinished homework. For me, it's Nick Berry's rendition of the *Heartbeat* theme. Just one note and I'm frantically searching for my school bag, despite being forty.

HMRC

Non-ministerial department of the UK government that takes all my money in January and then again in the summer.

Hot Cross Buns

Much like pancakes and mince pies, hot cross buns hold a special place in the hearts of the British yet are savoured primarily during a specific time each year. Which begs the question, do we really like them, or do we just stick slavishly to tradition? You tell me. Anyway, these spiced, fruit-filled pastries grace our tables each Easter – whether toasted and slathered in butter or enjoyed fresh from the oven, they're a beloved symbol of springtime indulgence. What? Do I want one right now? No, thanks; even though I love them, I'll wait until April, as is right.

Hay-on-Wye

Market town in Powys, Wales, famous for its bookshops and the site of the annual literary festival, Hay Festival, described in 2001 by Bill Clinton as 'the Woodstock of the mind'. Much better tea and cake facilities than Woodstock, too.

Horses

British people are very proud of their ability to a) move out of the way of emergency vehicles in a competent and timely fashion, and b) drive slowly and widely around horses. There's nothing as satisfying as that little wave from a horse rider to compliment you on a manoeuvre well executed.

Hadrian's Wall

When building of the 73-mile wall began in AD 122, it marked the boundary between Roman Britannia and unconquered Caledonia to the north. It's sometimes colloquially understood that the wall represents the Anglo-Scottish border, despite the wall lying entirely within England.

Haggis

Scotland's national dish. A delicious savoury pudding made from sheep's heart, liver and lungs mixed with oatmeal, onions and spices, traditionally encased in a sheep's stomach. Often served with neeps and tatties (turnips and mashed potatoes), especially on Burns Night.

In my opinion, it's what makes a full Scottish breakfast just that tiny bit superior to a full English. Some food historians argue that haggis originated in England, but the purpose of this book isn't to cause a war, so I'll leave that for you to investigate in your own time.

Harry Potter

Fictional young wizard. Since 1997 when the first book was published, HP and the gang have become a phenomenon that's left an indelible mark on Britain. Go to any old town or city in the UK, preferably one with cobbles, and you'll find a tourist looking up at an old brick building, saying, 'Wow, it's just like *Harry Potter.*'

Hull

Vibrant city (named UK City of Culture in 2017) in East Yorkshire, boasting stunning waterfront views and a rich maritime history. Another H, the nearby Humber Bridge, is one of the world's longest single-span suspension bridges. English mathematician, logician and philosopher John Venn, of diagram fame, is from here.

Insults

British people love insults so much, they can make literally any noun an insult purely by sticking the word 'absolute' in front of it. Two examples, which I've found by simply looking around my desk: 1. You absolute plant pot. 2. You absolute lamp. We're also masters of creating insults that require no swearing at all. Here are my top ten:

1. Dipstick
2. Plonker
3. Wally
4. Wazzock
5. Muppet
6. Spanner
7. Mug

8. Plank
9. Numpty
10. Pillock

Iced Buns

We took a hot dog bun, stuck some icing on it and called it a cake. British ingenuity at its best.

Inventions

Brits have come up with a hell of a lot of stuff in our time. I blame the rain, meaning a lot of time messing around with nuts and bolts in sheds. There are simply too many to list here, but some personal favourites: the toothbrush, the kettle, the World Wide Web, vaccines, the first practical telephone, the motor car, jet propulsion, the radio, the custard cream and withering passive aggression.

'I should really start thinking about making a move'

Brits will say this when they've been trying to leave your house for many hours.

'I'll let you get on'

Brits will say this when they've been wanting YOU to leave their house for many hours.

Isaac Newton

One of the most influential scientists of all time. He formulated the laws of motion and universal gravitation, built the first practical reflecting telescope and developed a sophisticated theory of colour, developed infinitesimal calculus and completely changed the way we think about everything. What a show off. You can visit Newton's apple tree, representing his theory of gravity, at his family home, Woolsthorpe Manor, in Grantham, Lincolnshire.

I'm a Celebrity ... Get Me Out of Here!

Minor celebrities go into a jungle, eat some animal genitals then come out again a bit thinner and a lot richer. Watched by millions.

Isle of Wight

Referred to as 'The Island' by its 141,000 residents, the Isle of Wight off the coast of Hampshire is the largest and second-most populous island (the first being Portsea Island, where most of Portsmouth is found) in England. As well as being where Very British Problems merchandise is made, it's also officially the sunniest place in the UK, according to the Met Office, with the seaside resort of Shanklin getting an average of 1,923 hours of sunshine per year, as compared to say, Manchester, which gets 35 seconds.

IKEA

Its origins are Swedish, and its headquarters are in the Netherlands, but it's a British person's favourite place to shop for economically priced flatpack furniture. What really draws Brits by the millions to IKEA, however, is the prize of a portion of cheap meatballs before going back to the car. The chain sells more than two million meatballs worldwide every single day.

Inverness

The UK's most northerly city, the cultural capital of the Scottish Highlands and also the nearest city (23 miles) to Loch Ness, home of Scotland's most famous dinosaur-like monster. Affectionately known as Nessie, the Loch Ness Monster has brought worldwide attention and tourism to Loch Ness since the 1933 report of George Spicer's alleged sighting of 'a most extraordinary form of animal'.

Ice Lollies and Ice Cream Vans

If the temperature gets above 12 degrees Celsius, then Brits are having an ice lolly, either from a shop or from a colourful, musical van that drives around housing estates delivering frozen goodness. But what's a Brit's favourite lolly? Well, it's either a Calippo, Magnum, Fab, Feast, Rocket, Fruit Pastille, Solero, Mini Milk, Twister, Nobbly Bobbly, Choc Ice, 99 with flake or something else entirely.

Imperial Leather

The bar of soap Brits grow up using, with its fancy flag printed proudly in the middle of the creamy bar. Good enough to eat. You can smell it right now, can't you?

Irn-Bru

Scottish soft drink invented in 1889. Tastes as alarmingly bright as it looks.

J

Jaffa Cakes

Brits have an undeniable affection for Jaffa Cakes.
Almost as much as we relish debating whether they
belong in the biscuit or cake category. McVitie's even
faced a courtroom showdown over this in a VAT
tribunal back in 1991. Successfully arguing its case,
the company presented a giant Jaffa Cake in court
(wish I was there with a giant cup of tea). The court,
while acknowledging Jaffa Cakes' dual nature as
both biscuity and cakey, ruled them legally as cakes,
exempting them from VAT in the UK. Their decision
hinged partly on the fact that biscuits go soft when left
out, while cakes go hard – and Jaffa Cakes do indeed
harden. Fascinating stuff.

Jacket (Light)

A Brit will seldom venture out without a light jacket, regardless of the scorching 40-degree-Celsius heat and clear skies. It's a precaution against unpredictable weather (see the W section), which has a knack for turning chilly or unleashing a downpour, often around 5pm. Even on the sunniest days, come teatime ('Cold when the sun goes in, isn't it?') you'll regret not having that light jacket handy.

Jumper

What the British call a sweater. As well as a light jacket, to be a true Brit you should always have one of these on you, too.

John Lewis

Is there a more quintessentially British establishment than John Lewis? Since 1864, it has been a cornerstone of British retail, offering everything from fashion and homeware to electronics and furniture. A John Lewis store in a town centre is a hallmark of prosperity. And in 2007, the company reinvented the Christmas telly advert, meaning that all big shops now release theirs like a much-anticipated mini movie, complete with breathless cover version of an 80s pop hit. They're all getting a bit samey now, but it wouldn't be Christmas without them. I mean, what else should Christmas be, if not a bit samey?

'Just these, please'

A Brit finds it impossible to place anything on a shop counter without saying, 'Just these, please.' The shop assistant will then still ask, 'Anything else?' whereon the Brit will reply, 'No.'

Jacket Potatoes

If you ask me (thank you, nobody ever asks me anything) the ultimate British comfort food is a jacket potato with butter, cheese and beans. A meal that can singlehandedly drag us through the long, cold winter.

Jermyn Street

Nestled next to Piccadilly, Jermyn Street epitomises London's posh charm, boasting a treasure trove of upscale men's attire. From bespoke suits to dapper accessories like hats and shoes, it's a sartorial paradise fit for kings (most of the buildings there are owned by the Crown Estate). And let's not forget the indulgent delights of Britain's oldest cheese shop, Paxton & Whitfield, serving up dairy delights since 1797. If ever I win the lottery, you'll find me strutting down Jermyn Street, adorned in finery, puffing on a Davidoff cigar, and nibbling on aged fromage like a true aristocrat.

Joking

Britain is celebrated worldwide for its rich comedic tradition. From sharp wit to absurd slapstick, British comedy spans a spectrum of styles, influencing global comedy trends. Its irreverent satire and penchant for the absurd have left an indelible mark on the world stage. On the other hand, *Mrs Brown's Boys* is one of our most-watched sitcoms.

Jam

Indeed, there's nothing quite as British as the sight of strawberry jam adorning thick white bread, raspberry jam cascading over a scone, or blackcurrant jam elegantly gracing a cheesecake. And let's not overlook marmalade, with its citrusy allure; while not technically jam, it shares the spirit of fruit preserves that defines British culinary tradition. Jam making burgeoned in nineteenth-century England, solidifying its status as a quintessential British export. We're also the country which brought the world the jam roly-poly, one of the all-time greatest gifts to the planet. You're welcome, world.

K

Kettle

The finest British technological invention, though it's not so much a machine to Brits as more of a deity, providing liquid nirvana at the click of a button. The first fully automatic kettle, the K1 from Russell Hobbs, was launched in 1955, and since then no British home has been complete without one. Kettle use is such a big thing in the UK that we measure electricity demand caused by its sudden collective usage during what's called a 'TV pickup' – the moment during a popular telly event when there's a break and Britain decides, as one, to put the kettle on. One of the biggest surges came at full time of England v West Germany in the 1990 World Cup Semi Final, when all of England consoled itself with going out on penalties by making a cuppa, causing a 2,800MW surge in electricity demand.

Kebab

Specifically, the doner kebab, of Turkish origin. British people (particularly drunk ones) have taken to doner kebabs like seagulls to discarded chips. In fact, two of the most-asked questions when you type 'kebab' into Google are: 'Why is kebab so popular in the UK?' and 'Is doner kebab British?' Usually served with salad and sauce ('Any sauce, boss?') in a pita or naan bread, you'll find doner kebabs spilled upon pavements up and down Britain every weekend. An easy way to tell if a Brit is properly pickled is to watch one eat a doner kebab – if they're also eating the paper wrapping, they've had one Jägerbomb too many.

Kilometres

Ew! No, thank you! We don't like them, get them away. In fact, get them MILES away, please.

Kendal

Market town in Cumbria, just on the edge of the
Lake District. Kendal is famous for its Kendal Mint
Cake, a dense sugary block flavoured with peppermint,
classically used by climbers and mountaineers as a
source of energy. The origin of the cake is allegedly a
batch of glacier mints that went wrong, with the boiled
solution turning cloudy overnight and confectioner
Joseph Wiper deciding it was good enough to eat
anyway. Its popularity increased with climbers after
the cake was taken on the Imperial Trans-Antarctic
Expedition led by Sir Ernest Shackleton.

'Kidding (You're)'

'You're kidding?' What Brits say when they hear
someone has died.

Kerfuffle

A delightfully British word (up there with
'flabbergasted' and 'discombobulated'), it means a
commotion or fuss. Example: A Brit trying to put a
coat on and accidentally putting it on upside-down so

all their coins fall out and then they bend over to pick them up and their trousers split up the backside could be described by them as 'a right kerfuffle'. Happened to me this morning, actually. Again.

King Arthur

What an absolute legend. No, literally, a medieval legend, rather than a real guy, who ruled Camelot with Excalibur, his magical sword. He's come to embody chivalry, leading the Knights of the Round Table in quests for the Holy Grail. Some scholars suggest he may have been inspired by a real British leader from the fifth to sixth centuries and has become amalgamated with mystical elements, like the sword, over time.

Kings Cross Station

Home to Platform 9¾, from *Harry Potter*. Tourists queue for hours to have their photo taken by . . . a wall. Magical.

Kippers

A whole herring, butterflied, then salted or pickled, and cold-smoked. Eaten for breakfast, most commonly, or sometimes enjoyed for supper. Very occasionally, someone will put them in the office microwave, and everyone will have to evacuate the room, leave the windows open for days and throw away the microwave after it makes everything else taste like fish (if you're reading this, Martin, what were you thinking?!).

Kilt

A Scottish garment resembling a knee-length skirt, made of wool and traditionally with a tartan pattern. Usually worn by a Scotsman or indeed someone with simply a very vague connection to Scotland who wants attention at a wedding.

Knightsbridge

Very posh area of London. Harrods, Harvey Nichols, lots of very fast cars even though the speed limit is 20mph. A good place to visit when you want to feel really poor.

L

Land's End to John o' Groats

Traversing the length of Great Britain between two extremes: Land's End in Cornwall, situated at the bottom of the UK map as England's westernmost point, and John o' Groats in Scotland, positioned at the top as mainland Britain's north-eastern tip. Covering approximately 814 miles via the shortest route, this iconic journey has enticed many to walk or cycle between the two points. Perhaps you'd like to try it yourself if you're tired of your usual stroll to the shops, though don't forget to wear your Fitbit else the 2 million steps won't count at all.

London Eye

Perhaps the safest way to take a leisurely rotation through the London sky (the only other way I can think of is 'falling'), the London Eye is Europe's tallest cantilevered observation wheel. It's the most popular tourist attraction in the UK – making it also the best place to experience a traditional queue – with over three million visitors annually.

London Marathon

Starting in Blackheath and finishing at The Mall, the London Marathon is the second-largest annual road race in the UK, after the Great North Run in Newcastle. It's basically a 26.2-mile victory lap, fuelled by determination and the promise of a well-deserved cup of tea/pint at the finish line. Since 1981, it's been a spectacle of sweat, tears, and the occasional outrageous costume. And let's not forget the charities, who've pocketed over a billion quid thanks to Britain's madcap runners (some of them dressed as hippos).

Love Island

Reality dating show where singles live together in a sunny villa and try to get off with each other. Watched by millions.

Liverpool

Much like the Cornish, Liverpudlians will say I've made a mistake featuring Liverpool in a book about Britain, as the city is not in Britain at all, but in the country of Liverpool. I'm not going to argue with them.

Litchfield

City in Staffordshire boasting the only medieval cathedral in Europe with three spires. And if that's not exciting enough, it's also the birthplace of Samuel Johnson, writer of the first authoritative *Dictionary of the English Language*, and of the grandfather of Charles Darwin.

Lies

British people tell lies, occasionally. Here are some common ones:

- 'I'm fine.'
- 'It's fine.'
- 'I didn't get your text.'
- 'That's nice.'
- 'I've had a lovely time.'
- 'I'll see you soon.'
- 'We should do this again some time.'
- 'That's interesting.'

Lighthouses

There are over 250 lighthouses dotted around the British Isles. Being an island, you need rather a lot of them (occupational hazard, you see). My favourite is probably Beachy Head Lighthouse, with its red and white stripes, which you can see in the 1968 film *Chitty Chitty Bang Bang* after the car falls off the cliff and flies for the first time. What's your favourite lighthouse? What do you mean you don't have one? Wait, don't go!

Leicester

Largest city in the East Midlands. Home to Walkers, the UK's largest grocery brand, which makes 10 million bags of crisps (see the C section ... quite enjoyable to say that, actually, 'see the C section') per day. Birthplace of ex-footballer turned pundit and online-opinion-haver Gary Lineker. Setting of my favourite books, the fictional diaries of British national treasure Adrian Mole.

'Look'

British people will start a sentence with 'Look' for one of six reasons:

1. They're quite cross.
2. They're a politician about to ignore a tricky question.
3. They're about to compromise.

4. They know they're wrong but have decided to double down/soldier on/change the subject.
5. They want someone to look at something.
6. They're Australian.

Luton

Did you know Luton was once a hub of straw hat production, with over 500 hat manufacturers in the Bedfordshire town during the 1800s? At one stage, in the 1930s, Luton was producing over 70 million hats each year. The club's football club, Luton Town, has the nickname, the 'Hatters'. Oh, and it also has an airport that's only an hour away from where I live, for when I want to subject myself to an EasyJet (see the E section) flight to Alicante.

M

Motorway Service Stations

The best part of any journey in Britain is pulling
into a motorway services and grabbing a hot drink,
a burger (even though it's 11am and you're on your
way to lunch), having a wee, considering buying some
camping chairs, and maybe having a quick go on a
massage chair or fruit machine. Enquire about a Brit's
preferred motorway service station, and they're bound
to have a response, maybe even a top ten. Personally,
I'm partial to Cobham, Killington Lake, Gloucester,
Tebay, Leigh Delamare, and Rugby. As for the bottom
of the list – well, let's not go there and risk making
enemies. I still might need an emergency Whopper
from one of these places.

Marmite

Sticky, dark brown paste (yum!) with a salty, powerful flavour. You either love it or you hate it, so goes the slogan. Personally, I love it. Did you know: it was actually invented by a German scientist, but let's keep that to ourselves.

Marble Arch

Erected in 1827, Marble Arch was designed by John Nash as the state entrance to Buckingham Palace but was relocated to the north-east corner of Hyde Park in 1851. From 1851 until 1968, three small rooms inside the arch were used as a police station.

Mind the Gap

Iconic warning heard throughout the London Underground (see the U section) since 1968. In 2013, an old recording of 'Mind the gap' by Oswald Laurence was reinstated at Embankment station, allowing the actor's widow, Dr Margaret McCollum, to hear his voice once more.

Mints

The first modern mint, Altoids, was invented by London confectioner William Smith in the 1780s with the purpose not of curing bad breath, but as 'a stomach calmative to relieve intestinal discomfort'.

Mint Sauce

The best sauce. Goes with literally everything. This is my opinion and I stand by it.

Modesty

Give a Brit a compliment, and they will tell you you're wrong. Try it. Tell a Brit you like their clearly expensive new coat. They will reply, 'What, this old thing? Oh, it's useless. It cost 2p. I found it in a bin.'

Magna Carta

Cornerstone of English legal tradition, inked by King John in 1215. It enshrined fundamental rights and liberties for citizens and put in writing that the king and his government were not above the law. Today, Brits playfully invoke it to defend quirky and sometimes belligerent behaviours, e.g.: 'It's my right to walk around the supermarket without a top on with my belly hanging everywhere when it's really hot, it's probably in the Magna Carta.' The power of history!

Marvellous

Could mean something is great, could mean something awful has occurred. See the S section (sarcasm) for more.

M&S

Home of Percy Pig, Colin the Caterpillar and delicious sandwiches (my favourite meal). Established in 1884, it's where the British like to treat themselves to a few nice bits. Probably where I spend 80 per cent of my wages. Also called: Marks.

'Maybe'

Means 'No'. See: 'Could do' in the C section for more detail.

Maldon

Town on the Blackwater estuary in Essex, famous for its distinctive Maldon Sea Salt which has been produced there since 1882. It's also the location of the first Tesco store to be designated as a supermarket in the country, established in 1958.

Manchester

Where British rain is made.

N

Nettles

The World Nettle Eating Championship (see the E section for more eccentric events!) is held in Dorset each year. Witness competitors bravely devouring up to 80 feet of stinging nettles, their tongues ablaze. Whether they resort to sucking on soothing dock leaves afterwards remains a mystery.

Nelson's Column

Erected in 1843 to commemorate Admiral Nelson's triumph at the Battle of Trafalgar in 1805, the towering Nelson's Column soars just over 169 feet high, serving as the ultimate avian VIP lounge for Trafalgar Square's pigeons. For a dizzying thrill, check out the nerve-racking footage of Blue Peter's John Noakes bravely scaling it in 1977 to help rid it of pigeon poo; it's enough to make you choke on your rich tea.

NHS

National Health Service. Formed in 1948. Get a bump on the head and go and get it fixed ... for free! Bit of a bargain to be honest.

New Year's Eve

In Britain, New Year's Eve festivities typically kick off with a bit of Jools Holland on the telly, followed by tuning into the midnight fireworks. After ensuring all doors are securely locked at quarter past twelve, it's off to bed. The next morning, a brisk walk is a must, along with exchanging cheerful 'Happy New Year!' greetings with hungover strangers. Rinse and repeat annually.

'Not on your nelly'

Meaning: certainly not. Cockney rhyming slang from the 1930s – a shortening of 'Not on your Nelly Duff' (whoever that is), to rhyme with 'puff', meaning the air of one's lungs. Any the wiser?

Notting Hill Carnival

Originating in 1966, this Caribbean culture explosion is Europe's largest street festival. Vibrant costumes, rhythmic beats, and delectable Caribbean cuisine define the event, celebrating diversity and unity with joy and exuberance. However, remember to attend on the Sunday or Monday for the full experience, otherwise you might find yourself stranded in a deserted street, as I did in 2019, because I went on a Saturday ... when it's simply not on.

Nibbles

Pigs in blankets, mini chicken Kievs, mini scotch eggs, mini sausages, mini sausage rolls, mini quiches, mini pork pies, mini samosas ... nobody does little nibbly bits quite like the Brits. Put them all together and you have yourself a 'picky tea', the best meal in Britain, enjoyed either at Christmas or when it's really, really hot.

National Lottery

Something I've never won, which doesn't seem very fair to me. Must be rigged.

Newcastle Brown Ale

English beer, affectionately known as Newkie Brown, sold since 1927. Brewed in Newcastle upon Tyne, it reigns as the top brown ale globally, even enjoying immense popularity in the United States. One of the first beers to be distributed in a clear glass bottle.

Norfolk

Nestled within Norfolk's charming embrace are vibrant cities like Norwich, historic gems like King's Lynn, coastal delights like Great Yarmouth, and idyllic villages with whimsical names such as Little Snoring and Great Snoring. The county is also the birthplace of many notable Brits, including Sir James Dyson (Cromer), Olivia Colman (Norwich) and, you may have heard of her, Princess Diana (Sandringham), to name but a few. Perhaps Norfolk's most famous son, however, is star of North Norfolk Digital, Mr Alan Partridge.

'Not quite what I had in mind'

What a Brit says instead of 'What the bloody hell is this?'

Nightclubs

Usually called things like Pulse, Lounge, Ocean, Liquid or Paradise, nightclubs in Britain are great places to stand around awkwardly until 2am shouting 'What did you say?' Behave with the slightest exuberance to get manhandled by a huge man in a black coat.

O

'Oh dear'

British meanings of 'Oh dear':

1. A minor hiccup has occurred. You've caught your sleeve on a door handle, or noticed a hole in your sock.
2. Complete disaster. Your limbs have fallen off, or you've heard news that an asteroid is heading to Earth that will imminently end all life.

Offbeat Museums

The Museum of Witchcraft and Magic in Cornwall, the British Lawnmower Museum in Southport, the Pencil Museum in Cumbria, the Dog Collar Museum in Leeds ... I could go on. Yes, Britain boasts a treasure trove of offbeat museums. These eccentric destinations celebrate the strange and fascinating facets of human history with gusto. Visit them and walk around with your hands behind your back, as is the proper British way to enjoy a museum.

Old Bailey

The Central Criminal Court of England and Wales, located in the heart of London, where many high-profile criminal trials have taken place throughout British history. If you find yourself standing trial here, you've been very naughty indeed.

Open-top Bus Tours

Popular sightseeing excursions in cities across Britain, offering panoramic views of landmarks and attractions. Buying a ticket for an open-top bus is also – along with hanging washing outside and washing your car – the quickest way to make it rain.

Oasis

Will they reform? Won't they reform? Has this book come out and then they've reformed and then split up again? Who knows? Will anyone ever stop asking? It seems not.

Olympic Stadium

Venue built for the 2012 Summer Olympics and Paralympics in London. It witnessed history as the stage for iconic Olympic moments like 'Super Saturday,' where three gold medals were clinched in just 46 minutes. Today, it serves as the home ground for West Ham United, which, for some, might not quite match the thrill of watching the Queen parachute into the venue in 2012.

Oven Chips

A British freezer is not complete without three things: half a box of ice lollies, three to ten loose peas rolling around even though you don't remember ever buying peas, and a big sack of oven chips. Here's how to measure the correct portion of oven chips:

1. Tip a suitable amount onto a baking tray.
2. Add a few more for luck.
3. Few more.
4. Few more.
5. There's only four chips left in the bag, might as well have them all.

Oliver Cromwell

Widely regarded as one of the most important figures in British history and one of the most polarising. During a visit to the Oliver Cromwell Museum in Huntingdon, his birthplace, I dared to ask an expert the ultimate question: 'Was he a goodie or a baddie?' The response? A deep sigh followed by, 'Now, that's a big question.' Regardless of where you stand on Cromwell, one thing is certain: his banning of Christmas celebrations in 1647 surely left many Brits wondering when they'd receive their annual haul of new socks and Lynx Africa gift sets.

Oxford Street

London's most famous shopping street. Arguably the most people-y bit of England's capital at any given time. Hell at Christmas. Makes non-Londoners who visit say, 'This is why I could never live in London,' even though nobody who lives in London lives on Oxford Street.

Oop!

Involuntary little noise a Brit makes when bumping into someone or when they accidentally try to pull a push door.

P

Pancake Day

'But you can eat pancakes any day of the year!' non-Brits cry, when they hear we have a dedicated Pancake Day. No, thank you, we shall do the British thing of waiting until the appropriate day, called Pancake Day, upon which we will eat pancakes until sick of pancakes and requiring of no further pancakes for another whole year. And they will not be fat, fluffy pancakes with maple syrup, certainly not! They will be thin and burnt, ripped and crumpled, after being thrown about a bit, and doused in horrible sour lemon, preferably artificial lemon from a plastic bottle that looks like a real lemon. It's just how we like it. Fun fact: Britain has a special Pancake Race in Olney, Milton Keynes, where since 1445, apron-wearing female residents of the town run a race with frying pans in hand.

Parks

Britain is indeed a green and pleasant land. There are fifteen national parks in the UK: ten in England (10 per cent of the land area), including the Peak District and the Lake District, three in Wales (20 per cent of land area) and two in Scotland (around 7 per cent). These huge parks are great for hikers and climbers, but we also have an abundance of medium-sized parks (for sunbathers and joggers) and smaller parks in housing estates (for teenagers to vape in). Without them, parkrun, founded in Bushy Park, London in 2004, which now takes place in over 2,000 locations, simply couldn't exist.

Paddington Bear

The last-known bear to have taken afternoon tea with Queen Elizabeth II. He's also responsible for hundreds of tourists visiting Paddington Station in London each year, who all, upon walking around the station for half an hour, sadly declare, 'It's just a station, really.'

Post Office

You'll see the Queueing section in the Q section.
Well, this is one of the places where that activity really
comes into its own. Once you do get to the front to
post your letter, after the chap in front finishes paying
in pennies, you'll be asked if you want special delivery,
signed for, guaranteed next day or something else. If
you're like me, you'll then reply, 'I don't know.'

Port Talbot

The powerful Welsh voices (and bodies) of Sir Anthony
Hopkins, Richard Burton and Michael Sheen all hail
from Port Talbot in Wales. It was also the home of the
Baked Bean Museum of Excellence, sadly closed in
June 2023.

Pork Pies

Who doesn't love a pork pie?! Well, me, for a start. But
loads of people in Britain absolutely adore a fat slice of
PP, perhaps with some piccalilli or Branston Pickle,
or my dad's favourite: HP Sauce. For the official stuff,
head to the town of Melton Mowbray in Leicestershire

for 'Protected Geographical Indication' status pork pies. Melton Mowbray is also one of six licensed makers of Stilton cheese. Great place for a picnic, or to get gout.

Pimms

Quintessential British drink made with gin, fruit and herbs, served over ice with lemonade and garnished with cucumber, strawberries and mint leaves. Particularly popular in summer, if we have one.

Peterborough

Regularly and rather cruelly voted one of the worst places to live in the UK, Peterborough in Cambridgeshire is mostly known by outsiders as being somewhere they once had to change trains on the way to or from London. People born there, like me, will sometimes plead, 'But it has a cathedral! Catherine of Aragon is buried there! And there's Queensgate, a big shopping centre that used to be all right!' But nobody ever listens.

Potholes

It's a bumpy experience, using British roads, so we have a special procedure for driving over a pothole:

1. Wince.
2. Tense everything, especially your bum.
3. Suck air through your teeth as you go over the pothole.
4. Shake your head and give the pothole a good frowning in the rear-view mirror; apologise to car.
5. Say, 'Bloody council.'

Pub Names

The naming of British pubs is a simple affair. You use an animal or bird (The Cock), a pair of animals (The Fox and Hounds), a landowner/royal (Duke of Bedford), an occupation with 'Arms' at the end (Carpenters Arms), a historic event (The Man on the Moon), something inspired by literature (The Moon Under Water), a myth or legend (Green Man), two words together (Boot and Shoe), a place name (Tavistock Inn), a plant or tree (Artichoke Tavern), the building name the pub is in (Lattice House), a service provided by the pub (Coach and Horses), a food (Stilton Cheese Inn), something to do with beer or wine (Barley Mow), a joke or pun (Pig and Whistle), something religious (Adam and Eve), a ship (Old Ferryboat), a trade or tool (Trowel and Hammer), something to do with transport (Railway Inn) or something else entirely. Like I said: simple. And the most popular pub name in Britain? Red Lion.

Q

Queueing

Queueing is a national pastime. The intricacies and nuances of British queueing etiquette alone could fill volumes, but, as we haven't much time, to simply provide a glimpse into the depth of thought and seriousness with which Brits approach queueing, consider this: When a fellow shopper politely enquires, 'Excuse me, are you in the queue?' it could imply one of the following five intentions:

1. 'This shop has a terrible layout, making it impossible to tell who's in the queue.'
2. 'I know you're not in the queue but you're standing in an odd place and causing everyone tension. I want you to realise this and move away from the queue.'

3. 'I know you're in the queue, it's just that you've decided to not move forward enough, leaving a large gap, and I don't like it at all.'
4. 'I just accidentally pushed into the queue, and I want to show you that I honestly didn't mean it. I am respectful of the queue, please believe me.'
5. 'I'm flabbergasted that the queue is so ridiculously long, and I'd like it known to all around me.'

Queen (the band)

If there's a large shindig going down in London town, something that the whole of Britain will be watching on telly, like a royal jubilee or the Olympic Games, then there's a 100 per cent chance Queen will be invited to play We Will Rock You, so look out for Brian May standing on a rooftop with his red guitar. It's just what we as a nation have come to expect.

Queen Elizabeth II

She reigned for seventy years and yet it still feels she was gone too soon. Come back, Ma'am!

Quality Street

A staple of the British festive diet, Brits subsist almost solely on Quality Street (as well as Celebrations and Roses) throughout December. First manufactured in 1936 in Halifax, West Yorkshire, they were named after J. M. Barrie's play, *Quality Street*. And the nation's favourite? It is, of course, the mighty Purple One.

Queensferry Crossing

This road bridge, which carries the M90 motorway across the Firth of Forth between Edinburgh and Fife, gets a mention in this book not just because there's not many British things that begin with Q (I heard you think it) but because it's the longest triple tower cable-stayed bridge in the world, so there.

Quiet Carriage

A single compartment on some British trains where passengers are encouraged to refrain from making noise, particularly on electronic devices. Tradition states there will always be one bloke in this carriage who's shouting into a mobile phone, while fellow Brits do their best to shut him up by staring furiously at the 'Quiet Carriage' sign and imperceptibly shaking their heads.

Quay Street

Street in Manchester that was home to Granada Television and the location of the *Coronation Street* set for the first fifty-three years of the show's production.

Quizzes

Brits love a quiz, whether it's in book form (and if you want two very good quiz books, check out the *Very British Problems Quiz Book* and the *Very British Problems Christmas Quiz Book*), on telly, on the radio, at the pub, via board games ... We're a nation of clever clogs. If we get a question right on *Only Connect*, we feel quietly smug about it for a week. Why do we love quizzes so? Because they combine all our faves: nostalgia, being right, arguing and, if in a pub, drinking.

Q (James Bond)

Here's a quiz question for you: What does Q, the name of the character in MI6 who supplies James Bond with his spy gadgets, stand for? The answer is quartermaster, which is not his name but his job title.

Quiche Lorraine

Or as I like to call it: British Pizza. Fine <sigh>, technically it's French, but it's safe to say Britain has heartily adopted it as a lunchtime staple. Perhaps we like quiche Lorraine so much because it's basically a fry-up that's easy to carry.

Quince Jelly

A traditional British preserve made from quince fruit and quite simply the best accompaniment to cheese that exists. Yes, better than chutney.

R

Rain

Cats and dogs. Tipping it down. Chucking it down. Pouring down. Spitting! We have so many terms for rain because Britain is, to put it mildly, wetter than an otter's pocket. (The Otter's Pocket is also the name of a pub, in Stamford. See the P section for more on pubs.)

How to really enjoy the rain like a Brit:

1. Stand at the window (inside).
2. Put non-tea drinking hand on hip.
3. Sip tea from mug.

4. Mutter 'Look at that rain', 'It's really coming down now' or 'The garden needs it'.
5. Say 'Good job we got the cushions/washing in' unless you didn't, in which case run out and get it.
6. Eat all the biscuits.

Ripon

The only city in Britain that begins with the letter R, Ripon is the smallest city in Yorkshire and the third-smallest in the UK. A seat in Ripon Cathedral features a carving of a rabbit and a griffin, which is said to have inspired Lewis Carroll to write *Alice's Adventures in Wonderland*.

Royal Family

Family made famous by reality TV show *The Crown*. Live in various large buildings around the country. Wave a lot.

Robin Hood

The closest you'll get to the real Robin
Hood these days is the Robin Hood
statue beneath Nottingham
Castle, his arrow aimed
at the gatehouse and the
establishment inside.
Cast in thick bronze and
weighing half a ton, the
7-foot tall effigy of the UK's
most legendary outlaw
stands on a two-and-a-half
ton block of Clipsham stone,
so even old Robby H himself would have a hard time
nicking it.

Red

Red buses, red phone boxes, red post boxes and post
vans, Red Nose Day, the Red Arrows, red poppies, red
fire engines, Simply Red ... It's a fact: Brits like red.

Romans

The Romans occupied Great Britain from AD 43 to 410 and at least twenty-six of the current sixty-three cities in England and Wales, including London, or Londinium as it was known, were fortified *civitates* during the Roman era. Fun fact: Every town with a name ending in 'chester', 'caster' or 'cester' was once a Roman town. The oldest Roman city: Colchester.

Roast Dinner

A Sunday without a roast dinner is like a summer without sunshine (which does happen in Britain sometimes). Brits will argue to the death about the rights and wrongs of a roast, but what do we all agree is the absolute best bit? Well, a Very British Problems poll, with 42,812 votes cast, named roast potatoes as the ultimate ingredient, with 40 per cent of the vote, pipping Yorkshire puddings (38 per cent) to the top spot. Gravy (lashings of) came in third (12 per cent). And where in Britain does the best roast? Ask any Brit and they'll probably tell you the same location: their mum's house.

Robert Burns

Scottish poet and lyricist, also known as Rabbie Burns, who lived from 1759 to 1796. Widely regarded as the national poet of Scotland. Big hits from the man include 'A Red, Red Rose' and, of course, 'Auld Lang Syne' (absolute banger).

Rugby

A sport originating at Rugby School, Warwickshire, in the 1800s. Being forced to play rugby at school, as I was, has two possible consequences. Either you spend the rest of your life with your casual clothes being a rugby jumper, blue jeans and smart brown shoes, talking fondly about how you once downed twelve pints of Bishops Finger at Durham University and stole Bertie Anderson's trousers, or, like me, you never play or look at the game ever again.

'Right!'

What British people say before they do absolutely anything, from standing up to climbing Everest.

Rules Restaurant

Founded in 1798, Rules is described as London's oldest restaurant. It makes an appearance in the James Bond film *Spectre*, and features in novels by Graham Greene and Evelyn Waugh. When the restaurant was threatened with relocation in 1971, John Betjeman wrote to the public inquiry, calling it 'unique and irreplaceable, and part of literary and theoretical London'. I recommend the steak and kidney pudding with oysters.

'Roger that'

My favourite thing to say before I completely forget what I've just been told.

S

'Sorry'

No matter where you go in Britain, people will be saying sorry for something, including but not limited to:

- Being hit with a shopping trolley.
- Bumping into a cupboard.
- The mess in a clean house.
- Needing an ambulance.
- Someone being in their reserved seat.
- Having to squeeze by in a shop.
- Asking for the bill.
- Being short changed.
- Having a door held for them.
- Nothing at all.

Shakespeare/Stratford-upon-Avon

Shakespeare is Stratford's most famous son, with his 1564 birthplace being on Henley Street in the Warwickshire town. Not to be confused with the arguably less picturesque Stratford in London, home of the Westfield shopping centre, an extremely busy 2.6-million square foot retail complex which gave me PTSD after I was tricked into visiting it one December.

Stonehenge

Officially a 'prehistoric megalithic structure', which makes it sound more exciting than it is, and a bit like there might be dinosaurs there. Unfortunately, when I visited, there was just some big rocks. I looked at them and said, 'It's amazing how they managed to get them here,' as every single British visitor says.

Sandwiches

My favourite meal. Especially when they contain crisps. Did you know: The first ever pre-packaged supermarket sandwiches came from Marks and Spencer, with the very first one being salmon and tomato.

Seasons

The four seasons in Britain last as follows: spring – two months, summer – eight minutes, autumn – three weeks, winter – seven years (six of which are January alone).

Slang (Cockney rhyming)

Some examples: Apples and pears – stairs. Brown bread – dead. China plate – mate. Bubble bath – laugh. And if you have cause to use them all in one sentence, it sounds like you've had quite the day.

Sticky Toffee Pudding

British dessert consisting of moist sponge cake made with chopped dates, covered in a toffee sauce and, ideally, served with vanilla ice cream. If it's on the pudding menu, it's impossible to resist.

Sarcasm

British people sound sarcastic no matter what they say. Trust me. Go on, Brits reading this, try saying these without sounding sarcastic:

- 'That's great.'
- 'Good for you.'
- 'Have fun.'
- 'Fascinating.'
- 'Thanks for that.'

- 'Well done you.'
- 'Good luck with that.'
- 'Sounds thrilling.'
- 'What a shame.'
- 'Wow.'

You failed, didn't you?

Slough

A town in Berkshire, often presented as a grim, post-industrial wasteland, most famously by *The Office*, but actually has strong transport links and a shopping centre described on Tripadvisor as 'quite depressing but OK'.

Sherlock Holmes

Solved crimes while wearing a hat.

Scones

Perhaps the biggest dividing point in Britain – jam first (the Cornish method) or cream first (the Devon method)? But does it really matter? Surely once the scone is in your mouth it all just tastes delicious regardless? Well, the answer is, yes of course it bloody matters. Few things matter more. And the correct answer is ... oh, I've run out of space.

Strictly Come Dancing

Celebrities learn to dance and get judged and eliminated each week. Watched by millions.

T

Tea

Brits have three essentials in order to stay alive:
air, food, and tea. Tea to Brits is what spinach is to
Popeye – our magical elixir, our strength for facing
life's absurdities. It's not just a beverage; it's our
liquid courage for navigating awkward conversations,
surviving office meetings, and enduring long chats on

the sofa with distant relatives. It makes the day that little bit more manageable. We use tea to celebrate, to commiserate, to pass the time, to catch up with old friends, to quash arguments, to soothe troubled minds, to toast achievements, to live! It's simply the best liquid known to man. Two topics Brits will fight to the death about: the correct way to make a cup of tea, and the best brand of tea. Let's not even go there.

Tunnock's Teacakes

At the sight of the iconic red and silver foil of Tunnock's Teacakes, Brits are enveloped in a wave of warmth and nostalgia, reminiscent of cosy afternoons on Nan's sofa. The shortbread biscuit, covered with a dome of Italian meringue (often mistaken for marshmallow) and a thin layer of dark chocolate, is the perfect accompaniment to a cup of tea when a biscuit just isn't going to cut it. Fun fact: These treats expand at altitude, making them a surprising snack for RAF Gaydon's V bomber crews, when one literally blew up on the instrument panel.

Trains

I recently took a fifty-minute train journey. It cost £38 and the train was late by twelve minutes. The fact I considered this a win tells you all you need to know about the British rail service.

Time Estimates

- 'Give me one sec' – Within the hour.
- 'I'll be one minute' – An hour or two.
- 'I'm on it' – Maybe today.
- 'In a bit' – Sometime this week.
- 'It's on my list' – Perhaps this month.
- 'Leave it with me' – Possibly never.
- 'If I have time' – Never.

Trifle

Layered British dessert, usually with sponge, sherry, a fruit element (fresh or jelly), custard and cream, served in a glass bowl/dish. First appeared in cookery books in the sixteenth century. Italy has a similar dessert known as *zuppa inglese*, translated as 'English soup'.

(Royal) Tunbridge Wells

Nestled in Kent, Tunbridge Wells is renowned as the epitome of Middle England. 'Disgusted of Tunbridge Wells' is a generic name used in the UK for an individual with staunchly conservative political views who frequently expresses moral outrage through letters to newspapers.

Tim Berners-Lee (Sir)

British computer scientist who invented the World Wide Web, the HTML mark language, the URL system, and HTTP. Not a bad CV, really. Named in *Time* magazine's 100 Most Important People of the 20th Century.

Tower of London

Historic fortress and UNESCO World Heritage Site. Served as a royal palace, prison and treasury. Built by William the Conqueror in 1078, it's home to the Crown Jewels and infamous for its ghosts, including the spectral apparitions of Anne Boleyn and the

Princes in the Tower. See the Y section for information on Yeoman Warders.

(Chicken) Tikka Masala

Popular dish said to originate in Glasgow. Delicious. I'm eating one now. While I do that, see the V section for Vindaloo, another dish from the South Asian community adored by the UK. Now can someone please pass me that naan? Ta.

The Thames

At 215 miles, the River Thames is the longest river entirely in England and the second-longest in the UK, after the River Severn. Although I wouldn't recommend drinking a cup straight from it (though the treated version provides most of London's drinking water), it's actually one of the cleanest rivers that flows through a major city and contains 125 species of fish. It also has the longest riverside walk in Europe, from Gloucestershire to the Thames Barrier in London.

Torquay

Coastal town in Devon. Sandy beaches, palm-lined promenade, bustling harbour, charming Victorian architecture ... yet all I think about when I hear the name Torquay is Basil Fawlty's reply to a guest complaining they expected a more interesting view from their hotel room: 'But this is Torquay, madam.'

U

Understatement

Brits are the masters of understatement. If a British person says to you, 'I've felt better to be honest,' you should perhaps call an ambulance, as they're probably about to die. Perhaps one of the best examples of British understatement comes from Captain Eric Moody, on British Airways Flight 9, 1982: 'Ladies and gentlemen, this is your captain speaking. We have a small problem. All four engines have stopped. We're doing our damnedest to get them going again. I trust you are not in too much distress.' Moody described the difficult, poor-visibility landing that followed as 'a bit like negotiating one's way up a badger's arse'.

Underground (The London)

The London Underground – the world's first underground passenger railway, in operation since 1863. With an annual ridership of over 1 billion people, you can perhaps forgive some of the seats for looking grimier than Albert Steptoe's underpants. Aside from being a wonderfully efficient and cost-effective way to navigate the capital, it's also a good place for forgetting personal items, with TFL reporting over 7,000 of our next entry left on their tube trains every year ...

Umbrellas

Yes! Over 7,000 umbrellas, lost on the underground network each year (four of those will be mine). The sturdy (and sometimes not so sturdy) brolly is the must-have accessory for every Brit. They're not just for shielding from the weather, they can also be used as a walking stick, a weapon of attack, for self-defence, for pointing at things, for tour guide instructors to lead the way and for twizzling round when doing impromptu performances of 'Singin' in the Rain'. Fun fact: National Umbrella Day is on 10 February.

Ulverston

Market town in Cumbria. As Stan Laurel's birthplace, it's home to the Laurel and Hardy Museum.

Universities

There are 166 universities in the UK with, at time of writing, seven of them in the worldwide top fifty – and the University of Oxford nabbing the top spot! So, these isles are a great place to study. Personally, I don't remember much studying at university, but I did learn how to feed myself for £20 a week, knowledge which, as a comedy author, has continued to come in very handy.

University Challenge

First airing on British television in 1962, *University Challenge* is the quiz that, for over sixty years, has been making Brits feel smug after getting one question right per episode. In 2017 I watched an episode and got four correct answers in a row and seriously considered changing my name to Einstein. I still tell people about it, as you can see.

Underdogs

Brits love a plucky underdog. But as soon as that underdog triumphs and becomes a top dog, then we don't like them any more. For proof of this, see the British media's treatment of anyone successful.

UK Parliament

Essentially a collection of people who argue a lot for the purpose of democratically making the life of the British public better. Spoiler: It rarely, if ever, gets better. 'The next lot will probably be better,' Brits say, every year of their adult lives. Still ... mustn't grumble.

Uppingham

Market town in the county of Rutland, voted best place to live in the Midlands by *The Times* in 2022. Perhaps best known for its public school, with famous graduates including Stephen Fry, Rowan Atkinson and Hugh Jackman. I went to rival institution Stamford School, and we beat them at U14 rugby.

'Up yours!'

Charming British insult.

V

Visitors

No, thank you! Not today! Do not 'pop round anytime' even though a Brit will cheerily tell you to do just that. And if a Brit does have visitors – <deep sigh> 'COME IN, COME IN!' – they'll spend the entire visit telling them to leave by saying one or more of the following things:

- 'Anyway, don't let me keep you.'
- 'I'll let you get on.'
- 'Right.' <slap their own thigh>
- 'Gosh, is that the time?'
- 'Goodness me, it's getting a bit dark now, isn't it?'
- 'What time's your train?'
- 'Well it's been lovely to see you.'

- 'What are you doing for the rest of the day?'
- 'Did you want another cup of tea?' <please say no!>
- 'I should imagine you want to beat the traffic.'
- 'I don't like the thought of you driving in the dark.'
- 'What are you having for dinner?'
- 'I can't remember, did you bring a coat?'
- 'Do you want a hand putting things in the car?'
- Simply yawning and looking like they want to die.

Viennetta

British ice cream dessert, with hypnotic rippling waves of sweet, icy pleasure, launched by Wall's in 1982. A UK advertising campaign uses the slogan, 'One slice is never enough', but I'd go as far as to say one whole Viennetta is never enough. And which flavour is the best? The only answer I'll be accepting is mint.

Village Fete

The mayor standing by a tombola and reading out the winner of a £25 gift card for B&Q, a stall full of homemade chilli jam, a lady selling wooden signs saying 'It's gin o'clock!', the smell of barbecued sausages and homemade cider wafting through the air, an out-of-tune brass band trying their best, the barking of the dog show contestants, kids going wild on a bouncy castle, the tug-of-war competition between the local pubs, someone who's forgotten the fete is on and is jogging through it all in running kit, soggy sandwiches, getting sunburnt and rained on at the same time . . . ah, Britain at its finest.

Vans (white)

Look out for white vans if you're visiting Britain. Similar to white Audis and all colours of BMW, they're not required to follow any rules of the road at all.

Valentine's Day Meal Deals

Whereas Valentine's Day in the UK may once have involved a romantic table for two at Pizza Express, these days it's much more about the supermarket meal deal. Two ready meal mains, two puddings and a bottle of plonk for £15? Yes, please! These romantic grub packages also have the huge added benefit of not even requiring a partner at all.

Victoria Sponge

Ooh, a lovely bit of Vicky sponge (which nobody before now has ever called Victoria sponge) is the perfect accompaniment to a cup of tea. And who do we have to thank for it? Only the inventor of egg-free custard, Alfred Bird of Bird's Custard fame. Not content with just making delicious custard, this legend also developed baking powder in 1843 (the Victorian era) enabling the incorporation of butter into the traditional sponge recipe, leading to the birth of the Victoria sponge.

Vauxhall

Area of London 0.93 miles south-west from the centre, named after medieval manor Fox Hall. Samuel Pepys mentions 'Fox Hall' in his diary on 23 June 1665: 'I took boat and to Fox Hall, where we spent two or three hours talking of several matters very soberly and contentfully ...' It gives its name to British car company Vauxhall, founded at 90–92 Wandsworth Road in 1857.

Vindaloo

The fearsome Indian curry dish originating from Goa and beloved by Brits. The spice lovers amongst us will sit down in an Indian restaurant, peruse the forty different choices on the extensive menu, and then say the same thing we've said to the same waiter for years: 'Chicken vindaloo, please.' The waiter will ask if we're sure, as it's very hot, and we'll say yes please, we like it hot. The rest of the meal is spent sweating and saying 'Blimey, it's a hot one today,' as if it's a surprise. 'Are you okay?' our dining partner will say, as we turn red and drip all over the place. 'Yes,' we reply, every single time, 'Hotter the better.' We're nothing if not predictable.

W

Weather

There's loads of weather in Britain, most of it different types of rain. We also have three days of 40 degrees Celsius where the whole country sticks its leg out of the duvet, one day of snow where every single train and road shuts down, and, these days, around forty-two differently named storms. Britain can even have every single type of weather known to humankind in the space of just one hour. Never a dull day.

Wheelie Bins

I have missed a lot of things in my life: weddings, funerals, important meetings, medical appointments, planes, trains and buses, but I have never, EVER missed bin day. The sound of a bin lorry's air brakes is enough to get me from being in bed to standing outside in my dressing gown and pulling a wheelie bin in under two seconds. Wheelie bins are the most important possession in a Brit's life. Put out your bin first, and the entire street will copy you. Get caught putting something in a neighbour's bin, the entire street will hate you. Risk putting an extra bag out by the side of your full bin, the entire street will feel nervous for you. Miss the first rescheduled bin day after Christmas and ... well, you might as well leave the country. Wheelie bins are serious business in Britain, it's life or death stuff. If there's ever a category five hurricane in Britain, people won't think about their houses blowing away or their cars being destroyed; their very first thought will actually be ... 'THE BINS!!!'

Wimbledon

District and town in south-west London, famous for the oldest tennis tournament in the world and for the Wombles: pointy-nosed, furry creatures who live on Wimbledon Common.

Waitrose

British supermarket that wins my coveted award for the most responsive of the self-checkout barcode scanners in any supermarket.

Wellington (Beef)

In my opinion, all meals could be improved by being in Wellington form. Curry Wellington, Fry-up Wellington, Pizza Wellington, Spag Bol Wellington ... any dish can instantly be elevated by wrapping it in puff pastry. Fact.

Wellingtons (boots)

No, not footwear wrapped in pastry, but a type of waterproof rubbery boot beloved by farmers, countryside people and urban people who want to look like countryside people. They came about when the Duke of Wellington instructed his shoemaker to modify the eighteenth-century Hessian boot. Most Brits have a pair somewhere in the house, either permanently muddy by the front door, hanging on some sort of hook, or getting chilly in the garage.

White Cliffs of Dover

Region of English coastline in Kent, facing France, with striking white cliff faces made of chalk. The National Trust calls the cliffs 'a symbol of home and wartime defence', with the white cliffs forming the first or last sight of Britain for those crossing the English Channel to or from continental Europe.

Worcestershire Sauce

A sauce made primarily of fermented anchovies, which I'm sure 99 per cent of consumers are happy to simply not realise. Goes well with jacket potato and beans, and also cheese on toast. A fun game is to write 'Worcestershire sauce' on a piece of paper and ask an American to say it back to you.

Woking

Town and borough in Surrey. Has a Pizza Express. Need I say more?

Wallace and Gromit

Since 1989, this plasticine pair have been entertaining us with their madcap adventures. Shot by Aardman Animations using stop-motion animation – one frame for every tiny movement of the models – each production is a painstaking process. According to IMDB, the feature length *The Curse of the Were-Rabbit* (2005) required 2.8 tons of plasticine and took five years to complete, with only three seconds of usable film created per day. Extraordinary. Just while we're on the letter W, Wallace's favourite cheese is another for this list: Wensleydale.

Welsh Rarebit

The two greatest foods – cheese and toast – get together in glorious harmony. Some recipes call for ale and mustard, some add wine or Worcestershire sauce, but ALL recipes are delicious because, essentially, it's cheese on bloomin' toast.

Whitby

Yorkshire seaside town. Author Bram Stoker's visit to Whitby inspired his most famous novel, *Dracula*. He discovered the name Dracula at Whitby's old public library and set part of the novel in the town.

X

X-rays

Well, I thought X-rays were a British thing but it turns out, like Marmite – rather embarrassingly (see M section) – they were discovered by German scientist Wilhelm Röntgen in 1895. That was my only entrant to the X section, too. Shame.

Moving swiftly on . . .

Y

Yorkshire Pudding

We have a lot to thank eggs, flour and milk for: not only have they given us pancakes (see the P section) but also the majestic Yorkshire pudding. The name first appeared in a 1747 book *The Art of Cookery made Plain and Easy* by Hannah Glasse, who renamed the original version, known as Dripping Pudding. Once relegated to the role of a humble appetiser, designed to stave off hunger and make the expensive meats of later courses stretch a little further, Yorkshire puddings of yore were rather flat in comparison. However, in contemporary times, it's all about the rise, with Brits vying to create the loftiest and most expansive puddings imaginable. But how high should a Yorkie be? Well, in 2008, the Royal Society of Chemistry suggested, 'A Yorkshire pudding isn't a Yorkshire pudding if it is less than four inches (10cm) tall.' Still, they're all the same to me; if they're a bit on the flat side I simply use them as an edible plate.

York

City steeped in history, boasting stunning medieval architecture and winding cobblestone streets. Home to York Minster, one of the largest Gothic cathedrals in Europe, and The Shambles, a charming narrow street dating back to the Middle Ages. Additionally, it claims to have one of the most haunted streets in Europe, the aptly named 'Mad Alice Lane' (now known as Lund's Court).

Ye Olde Cheshire Cheese

Historic pub on Fleet Street, rebuilt in 1667 after the original pub burnt down in the Great Fire of London. Associated with prominent literary regulars, such as Dr Samuel Johnson, Mark Twain, W. B. Yeats, P. G. Wodehouse, Sir Arthur Conan Doyle and Charles Dickens (the pub features in *A Tale of Two Cities*).

Ye Olde Trip to Jerusalem

Another, even older pub, Ye Olde Trip to Jerusalem is a Grade II listed pub in Nottingham, which claims to have been established in 1189, the year Richard the Lionheart became king. One of several pubs claiming to be the oldest in England.

Yum Yums

Delicious sugar-glazed doughy twists. Incredibly easy to polish off an entire pack of four in the car, right before arriving home for dinner, and conveniently forgetting to mention it to your partner.

'You look well'

There are roughly eight British meanings of 'You look well':

1. 'You look well.'
2. 'You looked particularly bad when we last met and you've improved since then.'
3. 'You look larger than last time I saw you.'

4. 'We both know you're looking unwell but I'm trying to make you feel better about it.'
5. 'I can't remember who you are.'
6. 'You're sunburnt.'
7. 'You look incredible but I'm not going to go so far as to actually say that.'
8. 'I say this to everyone, regardless of how they look.'

Yeoman Warders

Ceremonial guardians of the Tower of London (see the T section), popularly known as Beefeaters, since Tudor times. Historically responsible for looking after any prisoners in the Tower and safeguarding the British Crown Jewels. All Yeoman Warders are retired members of the armed services and, rather fabulously, have their own pub, called The Keys (or the Yeoman Warders Club) in the Tower of London itself.

Yellowjackets

What Americans sometimes call wasps, but I've put it here because the W section was brimming full. So . . . Wasps: utter nuisances, aren't they? Step outside with a drink for a moment in British summer, and one of these pests starts divebombing you. 'Ooh, it's taken a liking to you,' someone blissfully unbothered remarks, as you dash around the garden cursing. Wouldn't be summer without them, though.

Yoghurt

Underwhelming weeknight pudding. Here's a typical after-dinner conversation on an unremarkable Tuesday evening in Britain:

Person hopeful for cake or ice cream: 'Have we got any dessert?'

'Yes, there's a yoghurt in the fridge.'

'Oh.'

'Yeah, go on then, just a quick one'

What a Brit says (while checking their watch) when asked if they've got time for one drink in the pub. They will then leave the pub at closing time.

'Yes, please'

What you should ALWAYS say when offered a cup of tea, even if you've just had one. Even if it'll make you need a wee. You never know when the opportunity will arise again.

YOLO

Meaning: You only live once. The only excuse you need to have another biscuit.

Z

Zizzi

Behold the triumvirate of passable high street Italian eateries: Ask, Pizza Express, and Zizzi. Oh, and Prezzo, sorry, I always forget that one. Venturing into Zizzi nearly two decades ago, I fancied myself impossibly sophisticated, as if I had ascended to a higher echelon and left Pizza Express in my wake. These days, that sensation is reserved for Franco Manca, but Zizzi still holds a special place in my heart. But now, a pressing question: Is it pronounced Zizzi like 'busy' or Zizzi like 'tee-hee'? I feel I'll never know.

Zebra Crossing

A pedestrian crossing, where vehicles are obliged to stop, allowing individuals to safely traverse the road. Despite the clear right of way, it's a uniquely British sight to witness a British pedestrian perform an embarrassed mini-jog across, accompanied by a small, apologetic 'Thanks, sorry' wave to the halted drivers.

Zoopla

There's nothing quite like the quintessentially British pastime of checking the current value of a house one used to call home, only to be filled with regret at the timing of its sale. And there's no better place to indulge in this nostalgic frustration than on property website Zoopla (or Rightmove, if you're that way inclined). You can also check if your neighbour's house is worth more than yours.

Zero Degrees

The temperature has fallen to 0 degrees. British people dare to put on their central heating for ten minutes. It costs £182.

Zoom Meetings

Or, more broadly, video calls. Since the onset of the pandemic, as a nation, we've become much more accustomed to conducting meetings via our computers. Despite the countless hours of practice, there's inevitably someone (usually me) who forgets they're on mute. Nonetheless, being on mute hardly detracts from the primary focus of video calls: assessing the current state of one's own hair.

Z (Generation)

Born 1997–2012. Know how to work computers a lot better than me.

Zoflora

In 2018, this disinfectant suddenly became the talk of the town, largely thanks to the endorsement of cleaning influencer Mrs Hinch. Before we knew it, everyone was rushing to buy it in bulk, and 'Have you tried the new Zoflora?' quickly became the most frequently asked question, especially from my mum.

Zetland Arms

Pub in South Kensington dating from the mid-1840s. In 1880, the landlord, Sid Chaplin, was the older half-brother of some film star or other, called Charlie.

Zucchini

Courgette. It's called a courgette.

Zennor

Village and civil parish in Cornwall, six miles north of Penzance. Mostly in this book because I didn't want it to end on 'It's called a courgette.'

ACKNOWLEDGEMENTS

Thank you to Juliet Mushens and all the gang at Mushens Entertainment, to Serena Brett and the team at Little, Brown UK, to my wife Sumin who had to listen to me asking 'does this make sense?' about every line of this book as I wrote it, to family and friends, and last but never least to all the good folks who follow Very British Problems. Now, I'm parched . . . someone stick the kettle on and let's all have a cup of tea and a biscuit, shall we?

If you enjoyed *Britain According to Very British Problems*, why not check out the *Very British Problems Quiz Book*?

A charming and challenging quiz book for anyone who values queueing, from the beloved Very British Problems brand.

Read on for a sample quiz . . .

FOOD AND DRINK

Boil the kettle, make yourself a cup of something warm (as long as it's tea) and crack open the Hobnobs to nourish your brain for these tasty teasers.

Q1.

Which of the following is a type of chicken dish, usually yellow in colour with the predominant flavouring of curry powder?

- **a)** Coronation Chicken
- **b)** Eastenders Chicken
- **c)** Emmerdale Chicken

Q2.

According to a Very British Problems (@SoVeryBritish) poll, which sauce most belongs on a bacon sandwich?

Q3.

In what month in Britain is National Yorkshire Pudding Day celebrated?

Q4.

What should you do with the last roast potato?

- a) Leave it to go in the bin, it's gone cold anyway and it's only a cooked potato.
- b) Wrap it in cling film and put it in the fridge until later.
- c) Offer it to everyone, hope everybody says no and then eat it yourself with any remaining gravy.

Q5.

A 'Snowball' is a retro cocktail, traditionally enjoyed at Christmas in Britain, containing which alcoholic beverage?

- a) Crème de menthe
- b) Advocaat
- c) Absinthe

Q6.

What sort of sweet is also the name of something shouted by Charles Dickens' character Ebenezer Scrooge, when he dislikes something that's generally seen as enjoyable?

a) Bah! Toffee!
b) Bah! Humbug!
c) Bah! Mint Imperial!

Q7.

According to a Very British Problems (@SoVeryBritish) poll, which meat is the nation's favourite when it comes to a Sunday roast dinner?

a) Chicken
b) Pork
c) Beef
d) Lamb

Q8.

According to the UK Tea & Infusions Association, how many cups of tea do Brits drink each year?

a) 60.2 million
b) 60.2 billion
c) 60.2 trillion

Q9.

Which brand of tea would you associate with chimps and the character 'Monkey'?

a)   Twinings
b)   Tetley
c)   PG Tips

Q10.

What is the optimum boiling time for Brussels sprouts?

a)   5 minutes
b)   5 hours
c)   5 days

Q11.

Which restaurant chain opened its first UK branch in Woolwich, south London, in October 1974?

a)   McDonald's
b)   Burger King
c)   Wimpy

Q12.

What was the name of the television show that first turned Jamie Oliver into a household name? It first aired in 1999.

a) *The Nude Cook*
b) *The Naked Chef*
c) *The Baker in the Buff*

Q13.

Which British soul band had a hit in 1975 with the song 'You Sexy Thing'?

a) Hot Coffee
b) Hot Chocolate
c) Hot Toddy

Q14.

According to a Perspectus Global poll in 2020, which flavour of Walkers Crisps was named Britain's favourite?

a) Smoky Bacon
b) Ready Salted
c) Cheese & Onion

Q15.

What type of meaty product would you expect to see hiding inside a Yorkshire pudding in the dish Toad in the Hole?

  a) Sausages
  b) Fillet steak
  c) Meatballs

Q16.

Traditionally, the British asparagus season runs from St George's Day on 23 April to what special day?

  a) Father's Day
  b) St Swithun's Day
  c) Summer solstice

Q17.

Which British band topped the UK charts in late 1968 with a cover of The Beatles song, 'Ob-La-Di, Ob-La-Da'?

  a) Marmalade
  b) The Jam
  c) Cream

Q18.

Bisto (you know, the gravy) is an acronym for:

a) Browns Instantly, Seasons and Thickens in One
b) Bastes, Improves Sausages, Tasty and Odourless
c) Best Indulgent Seasoning, Terrifically Opulent

Q19.

Who was on the throne when Marmite was created?

Q20.

Where in Wales does Tintern cheese originate?

a) Carmarthenshire
b) Monmouthshire
c) Pembrokeshire

Q21.

What is the most popular type of milk in the UK according to Statista.com?

a) Skimmed
b) Semi-skimmed
c) Whole

Q22.

The instruction to 'have a break' is linked to the subsequent enjoyment of which popular chocolate snack?

a) Twix
b) Mars Bar
c) KitKat

Q23.

What is the most popular pub name in the UK? A packet of pork scratchings for you if you get it right.

Q24.

Complete the title of the 1961 Roald Dahl book: *James and the Giant ...* ?

Q25.

Where did the Great Fire of London start in 1666?

a) Pudding Lane
b) Bread Street
c) Baker's Row

Q26.

What fruit sits atop the singles trophy presented to the winner of the gentlemen's final at Wimbledon?

- a) Pineapple
- b) Apple
- c) Banana

Q27.

When making a cup of tea, does the milk go in first or last?

Q28.

A barm cake is a ... what?

Q29.

What food is traditionally 'piped' into the room during supper on Burns Night?

Q30.

On what street in London would you find 'Rules', London's oldest restaurant?

- a) Brick Lane
- b) Maiden Lane
- c) Bear Lane

Answers

Q1: a, Coronation Chicken, created for Elizabeth II's coronation in 1953
Q2: Red/ketchup (61 per cent of the vote share)
Q3: February, since 2007
Q4: c, Eat it yourself, obviously
Q5: b, Advocaat
Q6: b, Humbug
Q7: c, Beef, taking 39 per cent of the vote share, followed closely by chicken (33), then lamb (19) and finally pork (9)
Q8: b, 60.2 billion
Q9: c, PG Tips
Q10: Depends entirely on who's cooking them
Q11: a, McDonald's
Q12: b, *The Naked Chef*
Q13: b, Hot Chocolate, and the song would hit the Top 10 in multiple subsequent decades
Q14: c, Cheese & Onion
Q15: a, Sausages
Q16: c, Summer solstice
Q17: a, Marmalade
Q18: a, Browns Instantly, Seasons and Thickens in One
Q19: King Edward VII in 1902
Q20: b, Monmouthshire
Q21: b, Semi-skimmed, by quite a margin. Stay middling, Britain.
Q22: c, KitKat
Q23: The Red Lion (closely followed by The Crown and then The Royal Oak)
Q24: Peach
Q25: a, Pudding Lane
Q26: a, Pineapple
Q27: I'll leave you to argue amongst yourselves.
Q28: It's a name for a bread roll. As is bap. Or bun. Or cob. Or a million other things Brits call a bread roll, depending on where they're from.
Q29: Haggis is led into the room by a bagpiper during the Scottish celebration
Q30: b, Maiden Lane